Shannon Sl

Biograpl.,.

The Inside Story of the Life,
Legacy, Accomplishments,
Personal Life and Career highlights
of a Former Football tight end.

Thomas C Sanchez.

COPYRIGHT.

TABLE OF CONTENTS.

INTRODUCTION

Shannon Sharpe, born on June 26, 1968, stands as a towering figure in the annals of American football. His journey from a humble beginning to becoming one of the greatest tight ends in NFL history is a tale of perseverance, triumph, and challenges. This biography delves into the various facets of Sharpe's life, exploring the defining moments that shaped his illustrious career and the subsequent chapters that unfolded in his post-playing era.

Early Life and Family Background

Sharpe's roots trace back to Glennville, Georgia, where he was raised in a milieu that would mold his character and tenacity. The crucible of his upbringing played a pivotal role in instilling the values that would later guide his professional and personal life. Amidst the challenges of a modest background, Sharpe's family became the bedrock of support that fueled his aspirations.

Childhood in Glennville, Georgia

Glennville, a small town with a tight-knit community, became the backdrop for Sharpe's formative years. Growing up in an environment that demanded resilience, he honed his athletic skills on local fields, laying the foundation for a future NFL career. The scarcity of resources and the struggles faced by his family etched enduring memories, shaping Sharpe's perspective on life and success.

The anecdote of a robbery, turned into a humorous recollection, reveals the resilience ingrained in Sharpe's character. His quip, "We were so poor, a robber once broke into our house and we ended up robbing the robber," offers a glimpse into the indomitable spirit that would propel him to overcome adversities both on and off the football field.

Sibling Relationship with Sterling Sharpe

The Sharpe household was not just the crucible for Shannon; it also fostered a competitive camaraderie with his older brother, Sterling Sharpe, a former NFL star wide receiver. The sibling dynamic played a significant role in shaping Shannon's athletic prowess. Their shared passion for sports became a common thread binding the family together, creating an environment where excellence was not just encouraged but expected.

Sterling's influence on Shannon extended beyond the confines of their home, impacting his early forays into sports at Glenville High School. The two brothers, each carving their niche in the world of football, shared a bond that transcended the gridiron. Their intertwined destinies in the NFL would later become a unique narrative, adding layers to the broader story of the Sharpe legacy in professional football.

Chapter 1: College Years

Shannon Sharpe's college years at Savannah State University marked a crucial chapter in his journey, laying the groundwork for his future successes in the NFL. As he transitioned from a small-town upbringing to the collegiate arena, Sharpe's athletic prowess flourished, and he emerged as a multifaceted sportsman.

Athletic Achievements at Savannah State University

Enrolling at Savannah State University, Sharpe embraced the opportunity to showcase his talents across multiple sports. His impact was not limited to the football field; instead, he became a standout athlete in football, basketball, and track and field. This unique versatility set the stage for a college career that transcended the boundaries of a single sport.

Sharpe's ability to excel in different disciplines showcased his exceptional athleticism and work ethic. It wasn't merely about being a football player; it was about being an all-around athlete. This distinction drew attention not only from his college peers but also from scouts who began to recognize his potential as a future NFL star.

Football, Basketball, and Track and Field

In football, Sharpe's talent was evident from the outset. His contributions on the gridiron were instrumental in elevating Savannah State's football program. As a tight end, he displayed a rare combination of speed, agility, and catching ability that set him apart from his peers. Sharpe's impact on the football field became a source of pride for the university, laying the foundation for a legacy that would extend beyond his college years.

Basketball provided another arena for Sharpe to showcase his skills. His presence on the basketball court was marked by the same determination and competitive spirit that defined his football career. The transition between sports demanded a level of adaptability that Sharpe effortlessly demonstrated, further solidifying his status as a true athlete.

Track and field added yet another dimension to Sharpe's college journey. Competing in jumping and throwing events, he demonstrated a versatility that mirrored his success in football and basketball. The discipline required for track and field complemented his overall athletic development, contributing to the well-rounded athlete he was becoming.

Records and Honors

Sharpe's impact at Savannah State University went beyond the field; it manifested in the record books and the accolades bestowed upon him. He became a three-time All-Southern Intercollegiate Athletic Conference (SIAC) selection from 1987 to 1989, a testament to his consistent excellence. The SIAC Player of the Year title in 1987 highlighted his dominance and influence in college football.

As a Kodak Division II All-American in 1989, Sharpe's achievements extended beyond conference recognition. The national acknowledgement affirmed his status as one of the premier players in Division II football. His leadership played a pivotal role in leading the

Tigers to their best records in program history, with notable seasons in 1988 (7–3) and 1989 (8–1).

In his senior year, Sharpe's individual statistics underscored his impact on the field. Catching 61 passes for 1,312 yards and 18 touchdowns, including three games with more than 200 yards, he left an indelible mark on Savannah State's football program. These accomplishments culminated in his induction into the Division II Football Hall of Fame in 2009, the university's athletic Hall of Fame in 2010, and the Black College Football Hall of Fame in 2013.

Chapter 2: Baltimore Ravens Interlude

The Baltimore Ravens interlude in Shannon Sharpe's illustrious NFL career stands as a distinct chapter that added both depth and achievement to his football legacy. After a decade with the Denver Broncos, Sharpe's journey took him to Baltimore, where he spent two seasons with the Ravens. This period not only saw him add another Pro Bowl selection to his name but also culminated in a significant triumph—a Super Bowl victory that added a shining jewel to Sharpe's storied career.

Two Seasons with the Ravens

Sharpe's move to the Baltimore Ravens in 2000 marked a significant shift in his career trajectory. Joining the Ravens for the 2000 season, he brought his wealth of experience and winning mentality to a franchise that was on the rise. The decision to acquire Sharpe proved to be a strategic move, as he quickly became an integral part of the Ravens' offensive scheme.

In Baltimore, Sharpe continued to showcase his exceptional skills as a tight end. His rapport with quarterback Trent Dilfer contributed to the team's offensive effectiveness, and his presence on the field added a layer of experience to a relatively young roster. Sharpe's impact went beyond statistics; he became a locker room leader, mentoring younger players and contributing to the team's cohesiveness.

The 2000 season was a standout year for the Ravens, and Sharpe played a pivotal role in their success. His contributions as a receiver and a veteran leader helped guide the team to a remarkable regular-season record and a formidable playoff run. This season set the stage for the crowning achievement that awaited Sharpe and the Ravens—the Super Bowl victory.

Additional Pro Bowl Selection

Amidst the success of the 2000 season, Sharpe's individual brilliance did not go unnoticed. His performances on the field once again earned him Pro Bowl recognition, marking an additional selection to the prestigious All-Star game. This Pro Bowl nod was a testament to Sharpe's enduring excellence, showcasing that even as he transitioned into the latter stages of his career, he remained among the elite at his position.

The Pro Bowl selection in 2001 added another accolade to Sharpe's growing list of accomplishments. It underscored his ability to consistently perform at a high level, irrespective of the team he played for or the stage of his career.

Sharpe's impact went beyond the statistical achievements; he continued to be a difference-maker on the field, contributing to the success of his team and earning the respect of peers and fans alike.

Super Bowl Victory

The pinnacle of Sharpe's tenure with the Baltimore Ravens came in the form of a Super Bowl victory. The 2000 season concluded with the Ravens facing the New York Giants in Super Bowl XXXV. Sharpe's experience in Super Bowl competition from his days with the Denver Broncos added a valuable layer of poise to the Ravens' roster.

In a game that showcased the Ravens' dominant defense, Sharpe's offensive contributions were crucial. His veteran presence on the field, combined with his playmaking ability, added a dynamic element to the Ravens' offensive strategy. The culmination of the season in a Super Bowl victory not only solidified Sharpe's legacy as a champion but also provided a fitting conclusion to his time with the Ravens.

The victory in Super Bowl XXXV was particularly sweet for Sharpe, as it marked his third Super Bowl title—a rare accomplishment in the NFL. His ability to contribute to championship-caliber teams with different franchises showcased not only his individual talent but also his adaptability and leadership qualities.

Chapter 3: Return to Denver Broncos

Shannon Sharpe's return to the Denver Broncos marked a homecoming for the veteran tight end. After a successful stint with the Baltimore Ravens, Sharpe rejoined the Broncos for the 2002 season, extending his legacy with the team where he had achieved much of his early success. This return not only demonstrated the enduring connection between Sharpe and the Broncos but also set the stage for a continuation of his illustrious career.

The decision to bring Sharpe back to Denver was met with enthusiasm from fans and pundits alike. His return added a familiar and seasoned presence to the Broncos' roster, and it signaled a commitment to leveraging Sharpe's experience and skills for the benefit of the team. The reunion with the Broncos set the stage for the next chapter in Sharpe's career, one that would see him build on the successes of his earlier years.

Continued Success and Records

Sharpe's return to the Broncos was marked by a continuation of his exceptional on-field performance. Despite being in the latter stages of his career, he showcased a level of consistency that solidified his status as one of the premier tight ends in the league. His connection with quarterback Jake Plummer and later with Jake's successor, Jake Cutler, contributed to the Broncos' offensive potency.

During this period, Sharpe continued to add to his already impressive list of records and achievements. He maintained his status as a reliable target in the passing game, consistently making impactful plays that shifted the momentum in favor of the Broncos. Sharpe's ability to create separation, make crucial catches, and contribute in the red zone became instrumental in the team's offensive strategy.

Notably, he reached a significant milestone during this stint with the Broncos—surpassing the 10,000 career receiving yards mark. This accomplishment solidified Sharpe's place in NFL history, making him one of the select few tight ends to achieve such a feat. His continued success was not only a testament to his individual skills but also to his work ethic and commitment to excellence.

Impactful Moments

Sharpe's return to the Broncos was punctuated by numerous impactful moments that etched his name in the franchise's history. His veteran presence and ability to deliver in critical situations made him a go-to player for key plays. Whether it was converting on third downs, making acrobatic catches, or providing a reliable target in the end zone, Sharpe's impact resonated on and off the field.

One of the standout moments during this period was his performance in the 2003 AFC Divisional Playoff game against the New England Patriots. Sharpe's clutch plays, including a memorable touchdown reception, played a crucial role in the Broncos' victory. The enduring image of Sharpe celebrating in the end zone captured the essence of his impact—a player who thrived in high-pressure situations and delivered when it mattered most.

Beyond statistical achievements, Sharpe's leadership became increasingly pronounced during this phase of his career. His influence extended to mentoring younger players, providing guidance in the locker room, and serving as a steadying force during challenging moments. Sharpe's impact on the team's culture and camaraderie was immeasurable, making him not just a statistical leader but a true team player.

Final Seasons with the Broncos

As Sharpe approached the twilight of his playing career, his final seasons with the Broncos were a blend of nostalgia and continued excellence. The 2003 season proved to be his last in the NFL, and Sharpe bid farewell to the game he had adorned for 14 seasons. His final years with the Broncos were a testament to his ability to adapt, evolve, and maintain a high level of performance even as the years progressed.

The decision to retire in 2004 marked the end of an era for Sharp as a player. His impact on the Denver Broncos was immortalized as he left the game as the all-time leader in receptions, receiving yards, and receiving touchdowns by a tight end. The records he set during his time with the Broncos stand as a testament to his enduring legacy within the franchise.

Chapter 4: Retirement and Transition to Analyst

Shannon Sharpe's decision to retire from professional football marked the conclusion of a remarkable 14-season career in the NFL. As one of the greatest tight ends in the history of the league, Sharpe's retirement in 2004 left a void on the playing field but opened the door to a new chapter in his life—his transition to a career in sports media and analysis. This transition not only showcased Sharpe's ability to evolve beyond the game but also solidified his presence as a prominent figure in the realm of sports commentary.

Decision to Retire

The decision to retire from professional football is one that every athlete approaches with careful consideration. For Shannon Sharpe, the culmination of the 2003 season brought a reflective moment in which he chose to hang up his cleats and transition to a new phase of life. His retirement was not just the end of a playing career; it was a pivot point that would redefine his relationship with the sport.

Throughout his 14 seasons, Sharpe had achieved unparalleled success, amassing records and accolades that secured his legacy. The wear and tear of playing in a physically demanding sport like football undoubtedly played a role in his decision. However, Sharpe's retirement wasn't solely about stepping away from the game; it was about leveraging his knowledge, experience, and passion for football in a new and impactful way.

Leading Statistics

As Sharpe bid farewell to the NFL, his statistical legacy stood as a testament to his on-field prowess. His career numbers were not just impressive; they were record-breaking. At the time of his retirement, Sharpe held the title of the all-time leader in receptions, receiving yards, and receiving touchdowns by a tight end. His 815 receptions, 10,060 receiving yards, and 62 touchdowns solidified his place among the elite in NFL history.

Sharpe's statistical achievements weren't merely about personal glory; they were a reflection of his consistency, work ethic, and ability to perform at the highest level over an extended period. His impact on the game was etched in the records he set, records that would withstand the test of time and become part of the NFL lore.

Transition to Media

Following his retirement, Shannon Sharpe seamlessly transitioned from the playing field to the world of sports media. His charismatic personality, deep understanding of the game, and articulate communication skills made him a natural fit for a career in sports analysis and commentary.

In 2004, Sharpe joined CBS Sports as an analyst for "The NFL Today," a pregame show that provided insights, commentary, and analysis on NFL matchups. This transition marked the beginning of Sharpe's second act in the realm of professional football, where he could share his wealth of knowledge and experiences with a broader audience.

His engaging on-air presence and unfiltered commentary quickly endeared him to viewers. Sharpe's ability to break down complex football strategies, provide insider perspectives, and inject humor into his analyses set him apart in the competitive landscape of sports media. His chemistry with fellow analysts further contributed to the success of the show, making it a staple for football fans on game days.

In addition to his role on "The NFL Today," Sharpe expanded his media footprint by co-hosting "Skip and Shannon: Undisputed" on Fox Sports 1 alongside Skip Bayless. The show, which premiered in 2016, became known for its lively debates, bold opinions, and, at times, humorous banter between the co-hosts. Sharpe's transition to sports debate television showcased his versatility and adaptability in the ever-evolving landscape of sports media.

Beyond traditional television, Sharpe embraced the digital realm, leveraging social media platforms to connect with fans and share his perspectives on trending topics in the sports world. His engaging presence on platforms like Twitter allowed him to maintain a direct line of communication with a diverse audience, further solidifying his status as a influential sports personality.

Chapter 5: Media Career

Shannon Sharpe's transition from the gridiron to the media world was a seamless journey that showcased his versatility and charismatic presence beyond the football field. Embarking on a successful media career, Sharpe became a prominent figure in sports analysis, engaging viewers with his insightful commentary, bold opinions, and dynamic on-screen persona. This exploration of his media career will delve into his significant roles on "The NFL Today" on CBS Sports, "Skip and Shannon: Undisputed" on Fox Sports 1, as well as his involvement with Sirius NFL Radio and other noteworthy engagements.

The NFL Today on CBS Sports

In 2004, Shannon Sharpe joined "The NFL Today" on CBS Sports, a pivotal move that marked the beginning of his media career. As an analyst on the pregame show, Sharpe brought a unique blend of expertise, passion, and a touch of humor to the broadcast. His insights into the day's matchups, player performances, and strategic analyses quickly resonated with viewers, establishing him as a trusted voice in football commentary.

Sharpe's tenure on "The NFL Today" was characterized by his ability to break down complex football concepts in an accessible manner. Whether discussing key plays, highlighting standout performances, or offering predictions, Sharpe's on-air charisma made him a standout presence on the show. His chemistry with fellow analysts added an entertaining dynamic, making "The NFL Today" a must-watch for football enthusiasts.

Beyond the Xs and Os of the game, Sharpe's candid and unfiltered commentary set him apart. He was not afraid to express bold opinions, providing viewers with a refreshing perspective on the personalities and storylines shaping the NFL landscape. His media presence was further enhanced by memorable catchphrases and an infectious enthusiasm that endeared him to fans.

Skip and Shannon: Undisputed on Fox Sports 1

In 2016, Shannon Sharpe took on a new challenge as the co-host of "Skip and Shannon: Undisputed" on Fox Sports 1, alongside sports commentator Skip Bayless. This sports debate show, known for its lively discussions, hot takes, and spirited banter between the co-hosts, became a staple for sports fans seeking engaging and entertaining sports commentary.

The dynamic between Sharpe and Bayless was a key element of the show's success. Their differing opinions, coupled with Sharpe's unapologetic defense of his views, created a compelling narrative that kept viewers tuning in. Sharpe's charismatic and animated style, combined with his deep football knowledge, made him a standout personality in the competitive landscape of sports debate television.

"Skip and Shannon: Undisputed" covered a wide range of sports topics, but Sharpe's football expertise shone through in discussions about the NFL. Whether dissecting game strategies, analyzing player performances, or sharing personal anecdotes from his playing days, Sharpe's contributions added depth and authenticity to the show. His passionate defense of certain players, teams, and his occasional debates with Bayless became defining elements of the program.

The show's format allowed Sharpe to showcase not only his knowledge of the game but also his ability to engage in nuanced discussions about broader societal issues intersecting with sports. His perspectives on topics beyond the field demonstrated a thoughtful and well-rounded approach to sports commentary, contributing to the show's broad appeal.

Sirius NFL Radio and Other Engagements

In addition to his television roles, Shannon Sharpe expanded his presence in the media landscape through Sirius NFL Radio. Hosting the "Opening Drive" morning program alongside Bob Papa, Sharpe continued to provide football enthusiasts with his unique blend of analysis, humor, and unfiltered opinions. The radio platform allowed him to connect with a diverse audience of NFL fans, further solidifying his status as a respected voice in the football community.

Beyond traditional media, Sharpe embraced digital platforms to engage with fans directly. His active presence on social media, particularly Twitter, provided a platform for him to share real-time reactions, commentary, and connect with fans on a personal level. This direct engagement showcased Sharpe's adaptability to the evolving media landscape, where social media became a powerful tool for sports personalities to connect with audiences.

Throughout his media career, Sharpe's engaging presence extended beyond traditional broadcast settings. He made guest appearances on various talk shows, podcasts, and contributed to sports-related publications. His ability to seamlessly transition between different media formats underscored his versatility and enduring appeal.

Chapter 6: Hall of Fame Induction

Shannon Sharpe's induction into the Pro Football Hall of Fame in 2011 marked the pinnacle of his illustrious football career. The journey from an unheralded seventh-round draft pick to a celebrated tight end culminated in this prestigious honor, recognizing Sharpe's exceptional contributions to the game. This exploration will delve into the significance of his Hall of Fame induction, the recognition and accolades that accompanied it, and other Hall of Fame honors that further solidified Sharpe's place in football history.

Recognition and Accolades

Before delving into Sharpe's enshrinement in the Pro Football Hall of Fame, it is crucial to highlight the numerous recognitions and accolades he amassed during his playing career. Sharpe's on-field accomplishments were not only impressive; they were record-breaking. As one of the most prolific tight ends in NFL history, Sharpe ranked third in tight end receptions, receiving yards, and receiving touchdowns at the time of his retirement.

Over the course of his 14-season career, Sharpe earned eight Pro Bowl selections, showcasing his consistent excellence and recognition by his peers and fans alike. His four First-team All-Pro nods and one Second-team All-Pro acknowledgment reflected the respect he garnered from the media and experts evaluating his performance. Sharpe's inclusion in the NFL 1990s All-Decade Team solidified his status as one of the era's premier players.

The Denver Broncos, with whom Sharpe spent the majority of his career, honored him by inducting him into their Ring of Fame and including him in the Denver Broncos 50th Anniversary Team. These team-specific recognitions underscored Sharpe's lasting impact on the franchise.

Individually, Sharpe's achievements extended to setting an NFL record for the most receiving yards in a game by a tight end, an impressive 214 yards. Notable playoff performances, including a 13-reception, 156-yard game, further solidified his legacy as a clutch player in crucial moments.

Pro Football Hall of Fame

The ultimate recognition for any football player is enshrinement in the Pro Football Hall of Fame. For Shannon Sharpe, this honor came in 2011, cementing his place among the game's immortals. The Hall of Fame induction ceremony in Canton, Ohio, served as a culmination of his extraordinary journey from Glennville, Georgia, to NFL stardom.

Sharpe's enshrinement speech was a poignant reflection on his life, career, and the individuals who influenced and supported him along the way. He expressed gratitude for his family, coaches, teammates, and the fans who played integral roles in his success. Sharpe's speech resonated with authenticity and humility, embodying the values that define a Hall of Famer both on and off the field.

His legacy within the Hall of Fame extends beyond the induction ceremony. Sharpe's bronze bust, forever immortalized among football legends, serves as a testament to his impact on the game. Visitors to the Pro Football Hall of Fame can trace Sharpe's journey through exhibits and artifacts that encapsulate the moments that defined his career.

Other Hall of Fame Inductions

In addition to the Pro Football Hall of Fame, Shannon Sharpe received recognition from other esteemed Hall of Fame institutions. His alma mater, Savannah State University, inducted him into its athletic Hall of Fame in 2010. This acknowledgment highlighted Sharpe's enduring influence on the university's sports legacy and his contributions as a three-sport athlete during his college years.

The Division II Football Hall of Fame also welcomed Sharpe in 2009, further celebrating his impact on the collegiate level. His record-setting performances and leadership at Savannah State University left an indelible mark, earning him a place of honor among Division II football greats.

In 2013, Shannon Sharpe received induction into the Black College Football Hall of Fame. This recognition not only emphasized his individual achievements but also acknowledged his place within the broader context of historically black colleges and universities (HBCUs) and their football traditions.

Each Hall of Fame induction added a layer to Sharpe's legacy, showcasing the breadth and depth of his impact across different facets of the football landscape. From the NFL's grand stage to college football's hallowed institutions, Sharpe's enshrinements solidified his status as a transcendent figure in the sport.

Shannon Sharpe's Hall of Fame induction was the crowning achievement of a remarkable football career. The recognition and accolades he earned throughout his journey, culminating in enshrinement in the Pro Football Hall of Fame, underscored his exceptional contributions to the game. The story of Sharpe's legacy is not just about individual accomplishments but also about the lasting impact he left on the teams he played for, the communities he represented, and the fans who cheered for him. His enshrinements in various Halls of Fame stand as a testament to his enduring influence on football at multiple levels, immortalizing him as one of the sport's all-time greats.

Chapter 7:Post-Playing Career Challenges

Shannon Sharpe's transition from the football field to the media landscape was marked by numerous successes, but it was not without its challenges. In the latter part of his post-playing career, Sharpe faced adversity in the form of legal issues, a defamation lawsuit, a high-profile home burglary, and a departure from the popular sports debate show, "Skip and Shannon: Undisputed." This exploration will delve into these challenges, shedding light on how Sharpe navigated through tumultuous situations while maintaining his public persona and professional resilience.

A. Legal Issues and Defamation Lawsuit

In January 2023, Shannon Sharpe found himself entangled in a legal battle when his former lover, Michele Evans, filed a defamation lawsuit against him in the New York Civil Supreme Court. The lawsuit claimed that Sharpe had spread misinformation about Evans, leading to damage to her character and integrity. Evans boldly stated, "This lawsuit is not just about seeking justice for the personal wrongs that I have endured. It's also about standing up to public figures who misuse their platforms to spread misinformation and harm others."

The legal proceedings brought a new dimension to Sharpe's public image, as the court of law became the backdrop for a personal dispute. For someone accustomed to the scrutiny of the media, this legal challenge presented a different set of hurdles. Sharpe's response to the lawsuit would not only impact his reputation but also shape the narrative around his post-playing career.

Navigating a defamation lawsuit requires a delicate balance between defending oneself and respecting the legal process. Sharpe's legal team likely worked to present a compelling case, emphasizing the complexities of personal relationships and the challenges of navigating public life. The outcome of the lawsuit would have lasting implications for Sharpe's public image and his standing within the sports media industry.

B. Home Burglary and Reward Offer

In May 2023, news broke that Shannon Sharpe's home had been burglarized, resulting in the theft of over $1 million worth of items. The incident, reported by several media outlets, added another layer of complexity to Sharpe's post-playing career challenges. The burglary not only raised concerns about the security of high-profile individuals but also thrust Sharpe into the spotlight for reasons beyond sports commentary.

Law enforcement investigated the burglary, searching for clues and potential leads. Sharpe, responding to the violation of his personal space, took a proactive approach by announcing a $50,000 reward for information leading to the arrest and conviction of the perpetrators. This public offer highlighted Sharpe's determination to address the situation head-on and seek justice.

The burglary not only had immediate consequences for Sharpe but also contributed to ongoing discussions about celebrity security and the vulnerabilities of public figures. Sharpe's decision to offer a reward showcased his commitment to resolving the situation while leveraging his platform to engage the public in the pursuit of justice.

C. Departure from Skip and Shannon: Undisputed

On May 31, 2023, it was announced that Shannon Sharpe would soon leave "Skip and Shannon: Undisputed" after reaching a buyout agreement with Fox Sports. This departure marked the end of a successful partnership with co-host Skip Bayless on the popular sports debate show that had garnered a substantial following since its premiere in 2016.

The announcement of Sharpe's departure stirred discussions among fans, media pundits, and industry insiders. The reasons behind the decision were not immediately clear, but speculation and rumors circulated about potential factors influencing Sharpe's exit. Such transitions in the media landscape often prompt questions about contract negotiations, creative differences, or personal motivations.

Sharpe co-hosted his last episode of "Undisputed" on June 13, 2023, bidding farewell to a show that had become a significant platform for his sports commentary and debates. The departure from a successful and widely-watched program raised curiosity about Sharpe's future endeavors and the factors that led to this significant career change.

Navigating the departure from a high-profile television show requires careful management of public perception and addressing the curiosity of fans and the media. Sharpe's ability to transition gracefully from "Undisputed" and communicate effectively about the change would play a role in shaping the narrative around this chapter of his post-playing career.

Chapter 8:Personal Life and Controversies

Shannon Sharpe, known for his achievements on the football field and in the media industry, has also been a subject of public interest regarding his personal life. This exploration delves into the intricacies of Sharpe's personal relationships, legal challenges, controversies, and the intersections of his private and public personas.

A. Relationships and Legal Challenges

Sharpe's personal life has occasionally made headlines, drawing attention to his relationships and legal challenges. One notable instance was in January 2023 when Michele Evans, Sharpe's former lover, filed a defamation lawsuit against him in the New York Civil Supreme Court. The lawsuit alleged that Sharpe had spread misinformation about Evans, leading to damage to her character and integrity.

Legal challenges of this nature can have a profound impact on an individual's personal and public life. The intersection of personal relationships with legal disputes adds layers of complexity, exposing private matters to public scrutiny. Sharpe, who had long been a public figure, found himself navigating the delicate balance between legal proceedings and the court of public opinion.

Relationships in the public eye can be challenging, especially when coupled with legal disputes. Sharpe's response to the lawsuit, both in the courtroom and in the public sphere, likely required careful consideration to protect his image while respecting the legal process. The unfolding of these events offered insights into the complexities of maintaining a public persona while dealing with personal challenges.

Beyond legal matters, Sharpe's relationships have occasionally surfaced in the media, providing glimpses into his private life. The challenges of sustaining personal relationships under the spotlight of fame add an additional layer of scrutiny. Fans and media outlets alike often scrutinize the personal lives of celebrities, creating an environment where maintaining privacy can be a considerable challenge.

B. Public Image and Media Interactions

As a prominent sports personality, Sharpe's public image has been carefully crafted through his interactions with the media. His charismatic and outspoken persona has contributed to both acclaim and controversy. Sharpe's media interactions, whether on television, radio, or social media, have played a crucial role in shaping how the public perceives him.

One notable platform where Sharpe showcased his personality was "Skip and Shannon: Undisputed" on Fox Sports 1. The sports debate show, co-hosted with Skip Bayless, became a forum for Sharpe's passionate and unfiltered commentary. His interactions with Bayless, characterized by lively debates and occasional banter, endeared him to some viewers while drawing criticism from others.

Social media has provided Sharpe with a direct channel to interact with fans and share his views on various topics. Twitter, in particular, became a platform where Sharpe expressed his opinions, engaged in debates, and occasionally addressed controversies. The immediacy and accessibility of social media can amplify the impact of public statements, making it a powerful tool for individuals in the public eye.

Controversies, whether arising from statements made on air or social media, have been part of Sharpe's journey. His outspoken nature has led to both praise and backlash, highlighting the inherent challenges of navigating a public image in the digital age. The dynamics of media interactions also underscore the evolving landscape of sports commentary, where personalities are not only scrutinized on traditional platforms but also in the digital realm.

Chapter 9: Legacy and Impact

Shannon Sharpe's legacy extends far beyond his impressive statistics on the football field. His contributions to the NFL and his unique impact on social media have left an indelible mark on the sports world. This exploration will delve into Sharpe's enduring legacy, examining his notable contributions to the NFL and the distinctive presence he carved out in the realm of social media and fandom.

A. Contributions to the NFL

wide receiver before transitioning to a tight end, he displayed adaptability and a commitment to team success. His eight Pro Bowl selections and four First-team All-Pro nods underscored the respect he earned from peers and the broader football community.

Off the field, Sharpe's leadership and impact were recognized by his inclusion in the NFL 1990s All-Decade Team, the Denver Broncos Ring of Fame, and the Denver Broncos 50th Anniversary Team. These honors speak to his enduring influence on the teams he played for and the league as a whole.

B. Social Media Presence and Fandom

In the digital age, a player's legacy extends beyond the field, and Shannon Sharpe has embraced the opportunities presented by social media to connect with fans and shape his public image. His presence on platforms like Twitter has become a distinctive aspect of his post-playing career.

Sharpe's Twitter feed is a vibrant tapestry of sports commentary, insights, and unabashed fandom. His tweets showcase not only his deep knowledge of football but also his willingness to engage with fans, critics, and current events. Sharpe's unfiltered and charismatic style resonates with followers, creating a unique space for sports enthusiasts to interact with a legendary figure.

Beyond traditional sports analysis, Sharpe's Twitter presence reflects his broader cultural impact. He shares perspectives on social issues, engages in friendly banter with fellow analysts, and injects humor into his posts. This multifaceted approach has endeared him to a diverse audience, expanding his influence beyond the realm of sports.

A distinctive element of Sharpe's social media engagement is his unwavering support for NBA star LeBron James. Sharpe's vocal admiration for James has become a recurring theme, earning him recognition as a dedicated and passionate fan. This aspect of his fandom has resonated with followers, creating a community of fans who appreciate Sharpe's authentic expression of sports allegiance.

The impact of Sharpe's social media presence goes beyond the virtual realm. He has successfully leveraged these platforms to connect with fans, share his unique personality, and contribute to ongoing conversations in the sports world. Sharpe's ability to navigate the digital landscape underscores his adaptability and continued relevance in an evolving media landscape.

Shannon Sharpe's legacy and impact transcend the traditional boundaries of a football player's career. His contributions to the NFL, marked by records, championships, and individual accolades, solidify his place among the all-time greats. Simultaneously, Sharpe's dynamic social media presence has allowed him to maintain a connection with fans, shaping his legacy beyond the confines of the football field. The intersection of on-field excellence and digital engagement defines Sharpe's enduring influence on the sports landscape and cements his legacy as a true icon in the world of athletics.

CONCLUSION

Shannon Sharpe's journey from a small town in Georgia to the pinnacle of the National Football League (NFL) and later to a prominent role in sports media is a narrative of achievements, challenges, and an enduring legacy. As we reflect on Sharpe's remarkable journey, we delve into the highs and lows, the records broken, and the impact he has left on the NFL and beyond.

1. Achievements and Challenges

Sharpe's achievements are a testament to his dedication, skill, and resilience. From his early days as a standout athlete in Glennville, Georgia, to his college years at Savannah State University, Sharpe displayed a rare combination of talent and determination. His transition to the NFL, despite being drafted in the seventh round, marked the beginning of a stellar professional career.

One of the defining moments in Sharpe's NFL journey was his time with the Denver Broncos. Winning two Super Bowls and contributing significantly to the team's success, he became a key figure in the franchise's history. His versatility, transitioning from a wide receiver to a tight end, showcased not only his athleticism but also his commitment to team dynamics.

The challenges Sharpe faced, such as the initial skepticism about his size and position, only fueled his determination. The transition to a tight end proved to be a strategic move, as he went on to break records and redefine the expectations for players in that position. His move to the Baltimore Ravens added another chapter to his legacy, winning a third Super Bowl and further solidifying his impact on the game.

The later phase of Sharpe's career, in the media realm, brought its own set of challenges and transitions. From being an NFL analyst on CBS Sports to co-hosting "Skip and Shannon: Undisputed" on Fox Sports 1, Sharpe navigated the complexities of sports commentary. Legal challenges, a home burglary, and a departure from "Undisputed" added layers of complexity to his post-playing career.

2. Enduring Legacy

Sharpe's enduring legacy is etched in the annals of the NFL and extends into the evolving landscape of sports media. His records as a tight end, numerous accolades, and Super Bowl victories have solidified his status as one of the greatest to have played the game. The impact he had on teams like the Denver Broncos and the Baltimore Ravens is ingrained in the history of those franchises.

Beyond the tangible statistics, Sharpe's legacy is felt in the intangibles – the passion, charisma, and leadership he brought to the field. His ability to make clutch plays in critical moments, as evidenced by his 96-yard touchdown reception in the 2000 AFC title game, is part of NFL lore. Sharpe's legacy is not just about the numbers but the moments that resonate with fans and enthusiasts.

In the media landscape, Sharpe's legacy continues to evolve. His outspoken and charismatic style on shows like "Undisputed" has garnered a dedicated fan base. His social media presence, marked by candid commentary and unwavering support for LeBron James, reflects a modern approach to engaging with fans and staying relevant in a digital age.

Sharpe's legacy also extends into the realm of representation. As an African American athlete and media personality, he has been a trailblazer, breaking barriers and inspiring the next generation. His induction into the Pro Football Hall of Fame in 2011 serves as a recognition not only of his individual accomplishments but of the impact he had on the broader landscape of the NFL.

In reflecting on Shannon Sharpe's journey, it becomes evident that his legacy is multifaceted. It's not just about the Super Bowls won or the records set;

it's about the resilience in the face of challenges, the ability to adapt and excel in different roles, and the lasting impact on the culture of the sport.

As Sharpe continues his journey in the media landscape with ventures like the "Club Shay Shay" podcast and appearances on "First Take," his legacy is in a state of continuous evolution. The ability to transition from a celebrated player to a respected commentator demonstrates a versatility that defines his career.

In conclusion, Shannon Sharpe's journey is a narrative of triumphs and tribulations, of breaking records and overcoming challenges. His enduring legacy is not confined to the football field or the television screen; it's a dynamic force that continues to shape the conversation around the NFL and sports media. As fans and enthusiasts reflect on his impact, Shannon Sharpe stands as an icon who not only played the game but left an indelible mark on its history.

Printed in Great Britain
by Amazon

46475171R00046